Moana
and the
Ocean

By **Heather Knowles**

Illustrated by **Annette Marnat**

To the wonderful people of the Pacific Islands:
thank you for inspiring us on this journey.

For my husband, Clayton: you have always been my ocean. –HK

For Tom –AM

AUTUMN
PUBLISHING

I have known Moana...

... since she was a child.

I have seen her heart.

I have felt
her spirit.

I have watched her grow.

I have felt her rhythm.

Step by step...

... I have seen her
reach great heights.

I have felt her courage.

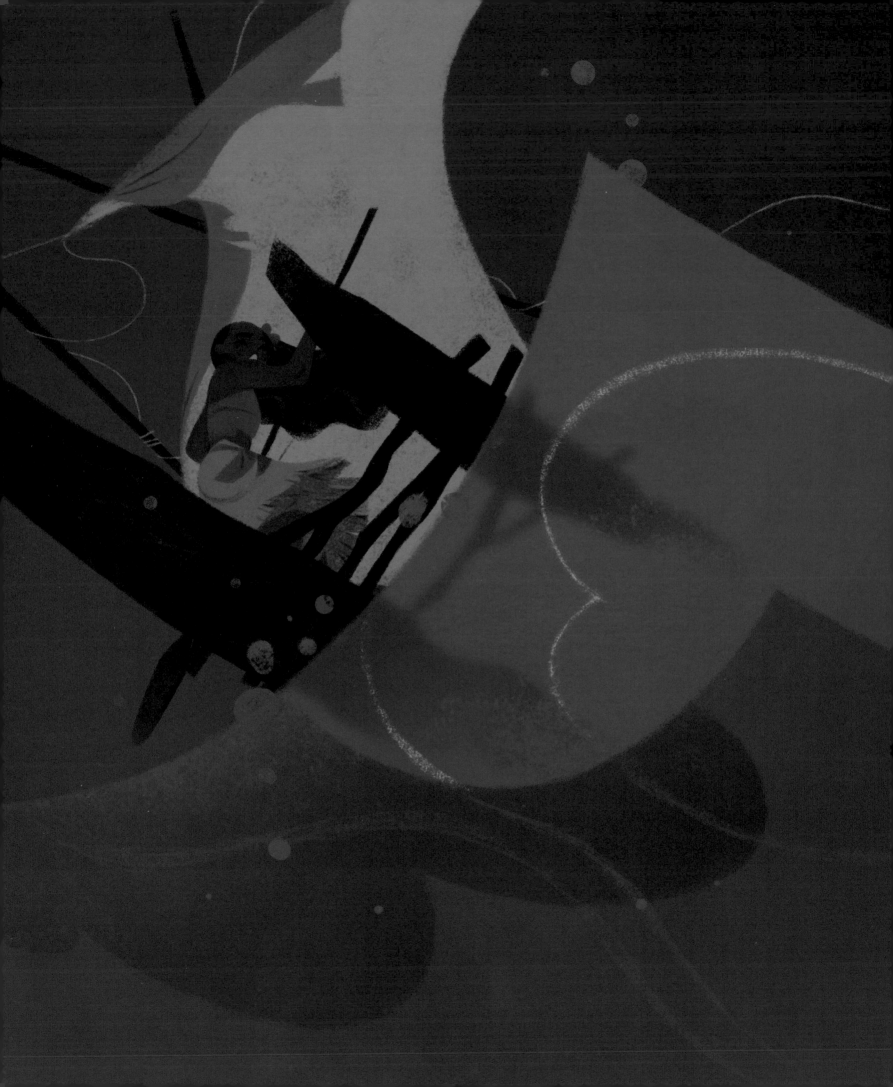

I have seen her struggle.

I have seen her fall...

... and rise again.

She is my

Moana.